Symbols of Canada

Trees

Edited by Deborah Lambert

Weigl

Published by Weigl Educational Publishers Limited
6325 10 Street SE
Calgary, Alberta
T2H 2Z9

www.weigl.com

Library and Archives Canada Cataloguing in Publication data available upon request.
Fax 403-233-7769 for the attention of the Publishing Records department.

ISBN 978-1-55388-923-6 (hard cover)
ISBN 978-1-55388-929-8 (soft cover)

Printed in the United States of America
1 2 3 4 5 6 7 8 9 0 13 12 11 10 09

Editor: Heather C. Hudak
Design: Kathryn Livingstone

Weigl acknowledges Getty Images as its primary image supplier for this title.
Alamy: pages 12, 13, 20, 22, 23 Manitoba, 23 New Brunswick, 23 Quebec, 23 Yukon.

We gratefully acknowledge the financial support of the Government of Canada through the Book Publishing Industry Development
Program (BPIDP) for our publishing activities.

Contents

Ontario

Northwest Territories

Saskatchewan

Prince Edward Island

Nunavut

Quebec

Yukon

What are Symbols?

A symbol is an item that stands for something else. Objects, artworks, or living things can all be symbols. Every Canadian province and territory has official symbols. These items represent the people, history, and culture of the provinces and territories. Symbols of the provinces and territories create feelings of pride and citizenship among the people who live there. Each of the ten provinces and three territories has an official tree or **arboreal** symbol.

Creating an Arboreal Symbol

In most cases, arboreal symbols are trees. In Canada, arboreal symbols are chosen from among the trees of the province or territory that they are meant to represent. Traditionally, the trees chosen as arboreal symbols are commonly found throughout the region they represent. However, trees that are not **indigenous** to the region may be chosen for historical reasons. Arboreal symbols can be recognized for historic, religious, cultural, or other reasons.

The leaf of Canada's arboreal symbol, the maple tree, is featured on the one cent coin.

Locating Provinces and Territories

Yukon

Northwest Territories

Nunavut

British Columbia

Manitoba

Alberta

Saskatchewan

Each province and territory has a tree symbol. Each province and territory is unique because of its land, people, and wildlife. Throughout this book, the provinces and regions are colour coded. To find a tree symbol, first find the province or territory using the map on this page. Then, turn to the pages that have the same colour province or territory image in the top corner.

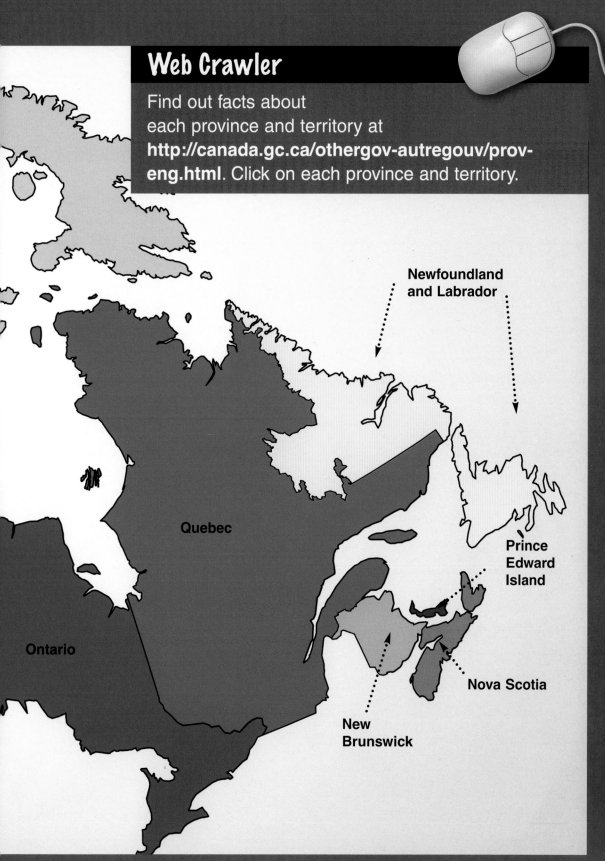

Web Crawler

Find out facts about
each province and territory at
**http://canada.gc.ca/othergov-autregouv/prov-
eng.html**. Click on each province and territory.

**Newfoundland
and Labrador**

Quebec

**Prince
Edward
Island**

Ontario

Nova Scotia

**New
Brunswick**

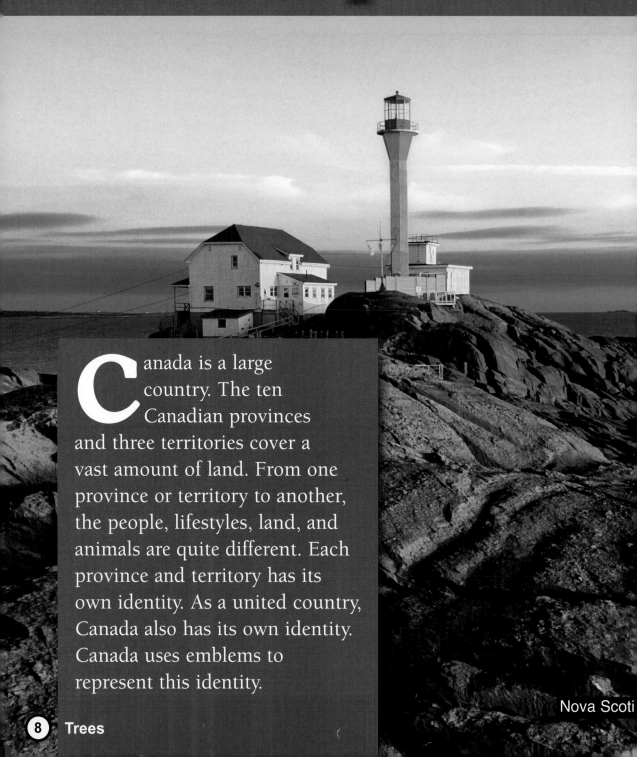

Canada's Land and People

Canada is a large country. The ten Canadian provinces and three territories cover a vast amount of land. From one province or territory to another, the people, lifestyles, land, and animals are quite different. Each province and territory has its own identity. As a united country, Canada also has its own identity. Canada uses emblems to represent this identity.

Nova Scoti

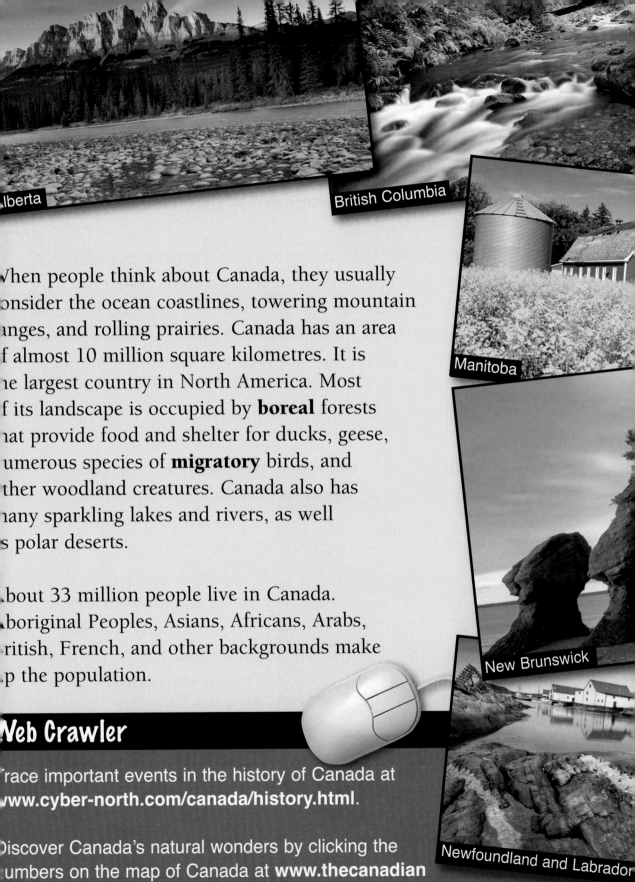

Alberta

British Columbia

Manitoba

When people think about Canada, they usually consider the ocean coastlines, towering mountain ranges, and rolling prairies. Canada has an area of almost 10 million square kilometres. It is the largest country in North America. Most of its landscape is occupied by **boreal** forests that provide food and shelter for ducks, geese, numerous species of **migratory** birds, and other woodland creatures. Canada also has many sparkling lakes and rivers, as well as polar deserts.

About 33 million people live in Canada. Aboriginal Peoples, Asians, Africans, Arabs, British, French, and other backgrounds make up the population.

New Brunswick

Web Crawler

Trace important events in the history of Canada at **www.cyber-north.com/canada/history.html**.

Discover Canada's natural wonders by clicking the numbers on the map of Canada at **www.thecanadian encyclopedia.com/customcode/Media.cfm? Params=A3natural-wonders.swf**.

Newfoundland and Labrador

Alberta

The lodgepole pine was named Alberta's arboreal symbol by the Legislative Assembly in 1984. This tree was chosen because it plays an important role in the development of the province.

This tall, slender tree is found mostly in the province's Rocky Mountains and foothills regions. The lodgepole pine grows 30 to 35 metres high and lives for 200 years. Its **evergreen**, needle-like leaves grow toward the end of the branches. Cones, which remain closed for many years, grow at the base of its branches.

In the past, Alberta's Aboriginal Peoples used the lodgepole pine as teepee poles. Early settlers used the lodgepole pine to make many items, such as railway ties and telegraph poles.

The lodgepole pine is still important to Alberta's forest industry. It is used to make fence posts and paper. The lodgepole pine provides homes for many wildlife species and protective cover for vital **watersheds**.

British Columbia

British Columbia adopted the western red cedar as its official tree on February 18, 1988. In the past, this tree played a key role in the lives of west coast Aboriginal Peoples. It is still a valuable resource for the province.

The western red cedar gets its name from the dark red colour of its bark. This **coniferous** tree is found in the moist coastal and interior regions of the province and can grow up to 60 metres tall. The western red cedar has scale-like, shiny, yellow-green leaves and egg-shaped seed cones. It also produces small, reddish **pollen** cones.

Early Aboriginal Peoples used the western red cedar to make many items. They made homes from the tree's wood, baskets from its roots, and clothing from its bark. It was also used for many medicines. The western red cedar is still used to make furniture, fences, and siding for houses.

Manitoba

The white spruce became Manitoba's official arboreal symbol in 1991. The white spruce was chosen as the province's official tree because of its extensive use by early and present-day peoples and its contribution to the province's development.

The white spruce is a coniferous tree that grows throughout Manitoba. It reaches 24 to 28 metres in height. The white spruce's four-sided, blue-green needles have lines of white dots on all sides. Although these trees can produce cones earlier, they typically start to seed when they are about 30 years old. Their seed cones range from green to deep purple in colour.

The white spruce is resistant to disease and usually lives for

about 200 years. Some have lived as long as 300 years. They are well-known as traditional Christmas trees and are often grown for that purpose. Aboriginal Peoples have used the white spruce to make bowls and pots.

New Brunswick

New Brunswick proclaimed the balsam fir as an official symbol of the province on May 1, 1987. Throughout New Brunswick's history, the balsam fir has been at the base of the pulp and paper industry.

The balsam fir is a small-to-medium-sized coniferous tree that can grow almost any place in the province. When fully grown, it can reach a height of 12 to 27 metres. The balsam fir's narrow, flat needles are dark green on top and white underneath. These needles are blunted at the tips. The tree's unique cones stand upright and are found on the upper side of one-year-old branches.

The balsam fir can live up to 200 years. Its wood is some of the best for making paper. Balsam fir is a favourite winter food of small mammals and various birds, such as the ruffed grouse. About 97 percent of New Brunswick's Christmas trees are balsam fir because of its soft needles and fragrance.

Newfoundland and Labrador

The black spruce, also known as the bog spruce, was designated as the official tree of Newfoundland and Labrador in November 1993. Although it is actually dark, bluish-green in colour, the tree is called the "black" spruce to distinguish it from other types of spruce trees.

The black spruce grows best in parts of the province where there is poor soil and bad weather. It is a slow-growing, small-to-medium-sized coniferous tree that usually grows up to 20 metres tall. Its dull blue-green leaves are **linear** and four-sided. The tree's egg-shaped cones are purple in colour when young, and they turn brown as they mature.

The black spruce is known as Canada's paper tree. For centuries, it has been used to make medicines and build birchbark canoes. Many types of birds, such as the spruce grouse, ruby-crowned kinglet, pine grosbeak, pine siskin, and crossbill, depend on the black spruce for food and cover.

Northwest Territories

The official arboreal symbol of the Northwest Territories is the tamarack. Found throughout the Northwest Territories, it was named the official tree on September 9, 1999, replacing the jack pine.

The tamarack is a small to medium-sized **deciduous**, coniferous tree that can reach a height of 10 to 20 metres. Although the tamarack looks like an evergreen tree, it has one important difference. While an evergreen tree keeps its needles all year, a tamarack sheds its needles every autumn. Its flat, soft needles are bright green in colour, and they turn a golden colour before they fall off. The tamarack is the only conifer that sheds its needles in this way.

The tree provides food for many animals. Deer nibble on the bark, squirrels store the cones for winter, and porcupines eat the sap. People can use tamarack bark to treat burns, and the sap can be eaten as a sweet treat.

Nova Scotia

Nova Scotia declared the red spruce its official tree in 1988. This tree was used by early settlers to build ships. Today, the red spruce represents the strength of Nova Scotia's people.

The red spruce is a strong coniferous tree that can grow in all types of soil to an average height of 25 metres. Its needle-like, yellow-green, shiny leaves are four-sided. They are curved, have a sharp point, and are found on all sides of the tree's twigs. The red spruce's egg-shaped, chestnut brown cones are about 3 to 5 centimetres long. These cones fall during their first winter or the following spring.

The red spruce can live up to 400 years. It is used for Christmas trees and to make paper. Early settlers used the twigs of this tree to cure a disease called scurvy. These twigs also can be boiled to make spruce beer.

Nunavut

Nunavut has not proclaimed an official arboreal symbol. Most of Nunavut is north of the tree line, where it is too cold for forests to grow.

In some parts of Nunavut that are sheltered from cold winds, tiny, stunted trees grow. None of the trees in Nunavut have needles. Instead, they have leaves. Trees that can be found in the province include the dwarf birch, Arctic willow, felt-leaf willow, least willow, green alder, and net-veined willow. Nunavut's trees and plants provide food for animals such as caribou, muskox, and Arctic hare.

Ontario

The eastern white pine was named Ontario's official tree in 1984. Commonly known as white pine, this tree was the basis of Ontario's early forest industry.

The eastern white pine is the tallest conifer in eastern Canada, reaching heights of 30 to 50 metres. Often, it is planted in areas that have been logged because it grows very quickly. Its dark, blue-green needles are clustered in groups of five. The needles are straight, flexible, and soft. White pine cones hang alone or in groups from branches. The cones have 50 to 80 scales and are usually found in spiralling rows of five. Soon after the cones become mature, they open and release winged seeds.

The eastern white pine can live to be 450 years old. This tree is important to wildlife, which feeds on its seeds, bark, and needles. It also provides shelter for animals, such as moose, bear, grouse, woodcock, songbirds, birds of prey, and small mammals. Today, the white pine is considered the most valuable softwood lumber. It is used for window frames, doors, and cabinet work.

Prince Edward Island

The red oak was adopted as Prince Edward Island's official tree in May 1987. The red oak is quite rare and can be found around Charlottetown, Tracadie, and Georgetown.

The red oak is a fast-growing tree that does well in nearly all well-drained soils. Red oak, best identified by its small capped acorns and **lobed** leaves with pointed tips, can grow up to 35 to 43 metres in height. The tree's leaves are pinkish white after budding. They turn into a deep and bright green colour by midsummer. In the fall, red oak leaves become a rich and dark, purplish-red colour.

The red oak begins to produce acorns after its second year. Though they are very bitter in taste, the acorns are eaten by birds, deer, and squirrels, making the red oak an important tree for local wildlife. It is also used for furniture, flooring, and woodworking.

Quebec

Quebec's official tree is the yellow birch. The people of Quebec chose the yellow birch because it was important to Quebec's early settlers and to the province's forest industry today. The yellow birch was named for its yellowish bark.

The yellow birch is a large shade tree that grows to a height of 18 to 21 metres on rich, moist, well-drained soils. This tree can be found throughout the province along streams, rivers, and upland slopes in mixed forests. The yellow birch is an **aromatic** tree, with a strong smell and taste of wintergreen from the buds and twigs. As the tree gets older, its bark peels into papery curls. On very old trees, the bark may become almost black and broken into flat plates.

The yellow birch is used to make furniture and hardwood floors. In spring, this birch can be tapped and the sap boiled down to make a wintergreen syrup. Throughout the year, its twigs can be steeped to make a delightful tea.

Saskatchewan

The white birch was named Saskatchewan's official tree or arboreal symbol in 1988. It is also known as the "paper birch" because the bark peels from the trunk in paper-like layers. Another name given to the white birch is the "canoe birch" because Aboriginal Peoples used this tree's bark to make canoes.

Most white birch is found in the northern three-quarters of the province. This tree grows well in cool weather and moist soil. It is common along watercourses and in moist wooded areas. The white birch tree grows quickly and may reach a height of 24 metres. Its unusual, attractive, thin bark is smooth and reddish-brown on young trees. As the tree matures, its bark becomes chalky white to silvery grey. In fall, the white birch's egg-shaped, pale-green leaves turn brilliant yellow.

The white birch can live to be 100 years old. It easily catches fire, but new trees can grow around the base of burned-out trees. Wood from the white birch is used for fuel, lumber, plywood, and **veneer**.

Yukon

The sub-alpine fir became the Yukon's official tree in 2001. It is common in many interior forests, usually growing at higher elevations.

The sub-alpine fir is a medium-sized tree that grows from 20 to 35 metres tall. In some cases, it can grow to 50 metres. This tree's short, stiff branches slope downward and do not break under the weight of heavy snowfalls. The blue-green needles of the sub-alpine fir have blunt ends that often have a v-shaped cut, or notch, at the tip. The needles tend to turn upwards, but a few may stick out from the underside of a branch. This tree's bark is smooth and grey, with **resin** blisters when young. As the bark ages, it forms into large scales.

The sub-alpine fir lives between 120 and 140 years, which is not long for a tree. The sub-alpine fir is harvested for lumber, plywood veneers, boxes, and pulp. Aboriginal Peoples use the tree's needles to make tea for treating colds. They also draw sap from the bark to make medicine for lung ailments.

Guide to Canada's Trees

THE NATIONAL ARBOREAL SYMBOL
maple

ALBERTA
lodgepole pine

BRITISH COLUMBIA
western red cedar

MANITOBA
white spruce

NEW BRUNSWICK
balsam fir

NEWFOUNDLAND AND LABRADOR
black spruce

NORTHWEST TERRITORIES
tamarack

NOVA SCOTIA
red spruce

NUNAVUT
no official tree

ONTARIO
eastern white pine

PRINCE EDWARD ISLAND
red oak

QUEBEC
yellow birch

SASKATCHEWAN
white birch

YUKON
sub-alpine fir

Canada's Arboreal Symbol

National emblems are symbols that are used for the entire country. The Canadian flag is one such symbol. Another is the common loon, which is the national bird. The beaver is the national animal. Canada's national tree is the maple. It has played a meaningful role in the historical development of Canada.

There are 10 types of maple trees in Canada, but it is the sugar maple that is most commonly thought of as the national tree.

The leaves of the sugar maple are 7 to 13 centimetres in diameter, and like all maples, turn red-gold in fall. When young, the sugar maple's bark is smooth and grey-brown. As it matures, the bark turns scaly and **furrowed**.

The sugar maple is known for its sweet sap. Each spring, sap is collected from the trees and boiled to produce maple syrup and maple sugar.

Arboreal Symbol History

Since 1965, maple tree leaves have been Canada's best-known symbol. However, the maple tree was not officially recognized as Canada's arboreal symbol until April 25, 1996. For many years, Canadians in the forestry industry requested that the government select the maple tree as Canada's arboreal symbol. They now use the maple tree as an official symbol when promoting Canada as a world leader in managing forests.

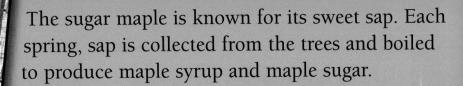

Parts of a Tree

Trees are an important part of our daily lives. They provide shade and relief from the Sun, and they replenish the atmosphere with oxygen for us to breathe. Trees come in many different sizes, shapes, and colours. Still, they all share the same basic traits.

LEAVES AND NEEDLES Leaves and needles are a tree's food factory. **Photosynthesis** begins when the Sun's warmth and light are trapped by green **chlorophyll** in the leaves.

ROOTS The roots are an anchor, holding the tree in place. The roots grow and spread out underground from the root tips. They form a huge network that draws nutrients to the tree and protects the soil from being worn away by weather.

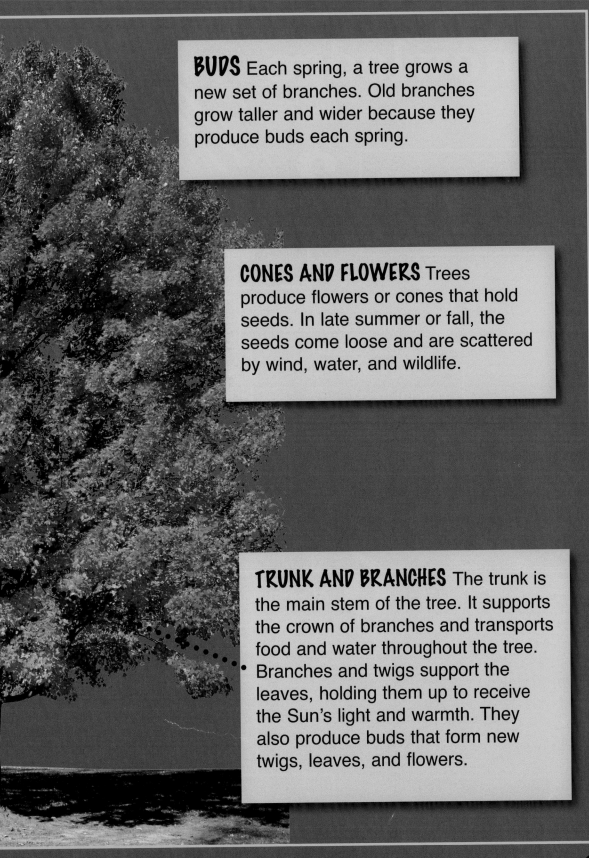

BUDS Each spring, a tree grows a new set of branches. Old branches grow taller and wider because they produce buds each spring.

CONES AND FLOWERS Trees produce flowers or cones that hold seeds. In late summer or fall, the seeds come loose and are scattered by wind, water, and wildlife.

TRUNK AND BRANCHES The trunk is the main stem of the tree. It supports the crown of branches and transports food and water throughout the tree. Branches and twigs support the leaves, holding them up to receive the Sun's light and warmth. They also produce buds that form new twigs, leaves, and flowers.

Test Your Knowledge

1 What is the national arboreal symbol of Canada?

2 Which official tree was used as a teepee pole?

3 In which province is the western red cedar the official tree?

4 When was the balsam fir proclaimed an official tree?

5 Which territory does not have an official tree as yet?

6 At what age does the white spruce usually begin to seed?

7 Which official tree sheds its needles in autumn?

8 What is another name for the bog spruce?

9 What is the average height of Nova Scotia's official tree?

13 Which official tree was named after the colour of its bark?

10 When does the red oak begin to produce acorns?

14 Which territory has the sub-alpine fir as its official tree?

15 Which official tree was used to cure scurvy?

11 Which official tree is considered the most valuable softwood lumber?

12 Why is the white birch also called the "canoe birch"?

Answers:
1. The sugar maple tree
2. The lodgepole pine
3. British Columbia
4. May 1, 1987
5. Nunavut
6. 30 years old
7. The tamarack
8. The black spruce
9. 25 metres
10. After its second year
11. The eastern white pine
12. Aboriginal Peoples used its bark to make canoes.
13. The yellow birch
14. Yukon
15. The red spruce

Create Your Own Arboreal Symbol

Create a tree symbol to represent you. Begin by thinking about what type of tree you like. Use this book to help you. What kinds of trees grow in the region where you live? Will your tree be coniferous or deciduous?

Think about how your tree will look. Will your tree be large or small? Will it have leaves or needles? Will your tree grow flowers? Look at the pictures in this book for help. You also can view more than 200 trees in Canada at **www.treecanada.ca/site/?page=programs_trees&lang=en**.

Draw your tree on a piece of paper. Use the diagram on pages 26 and 27 to help you design the parts of your tree. Colour your drawing with felt markers. When you are finished, label the parts of your tree.

Write a description of your tree. What kind of tree is it? Where does it grow? What does it say about you?

Further Research

Many books and websites provide information on trees. To learn more about trees, borrow books from the library, or surf the Internet.

Books

Most libraries have computers that connect to a database for researching information. If you input a key word, you will be provided with a list of books in the library that contain information on that topic. Nonfiction books are arranged numerically, using their call number. Fiction books are organized alphabetically by the author's last name.

Websites

Find fun facts about each of Canada's provinces and territories at www.pco-bcp.gc.ca/aia/index.asp?lang =eng&page= provterr&sub=map-carte&doc=map-carte-eng.htm.

Learn about Canada's emblems and other symbols at www.patrimoinecanadien.gc.ca/pgm/ceem-cced/symbl/index-eng.cfm.

Play online tree games and activities at http://arborday.net/kids/teachingYouth.cfm.

Glossary

arboreal: relating to trees

aromatic: having a strong, pleasant smell

boreal: northern regions with very cold temperatures

chlorophyll: a green pigment that absorbs light to produce energy

coniferous: trees bearing cones and evergreen leaves

deciduous: shedding leaves at the end of a growing season

evergreen: having green leaves or needles all year

furrowed: having long, narrow, shallow, grooves or wrinkles in a surface

indigenous: occurring naturally in a certain place

linear: extending in a straight line

lobed: having deeply indented margins not entirely separate from each other

migratory: to move from one place to another

photosynthesis: to use sunlight to make food from carbon dioxide and water

pollen: a fine, powdery substance that plants use to reproduce

resin: a solid or semisolid substance obtained from certain plants

veneer: a thin layer of wood used to cover the surface of something

watersheds: areas that are drained by a body of water

Index